EDGE
BOOKS™

Survival Guides

How to Survive Being
Lost at Sea

by Tim O'Shei

Consultant: Al Siebert, PhD
Author of *The Survivor Personality*

Capstone
press®
Mankato, Minnesota

Edge Books are published by Capstone Press,
151 Good Counsel Drive, P.O. Box 669, Mankato, Minnesota 56002.
www.capstonepress.com

Library of Congress Cataloging-in-Publication Data
O'Shei, Tim.
    How to survive being lost at sea / by Tim O'Shei.
    p. cm. — (Edge books. Prepare to Survive)
    Includes bibliographical references and index.
    ISBN-13: 978-1-4296-2280-6 (hardcover)
    ISBN-10: 1-4296-2280-6 (hardcover)
    1. Shipwrecks — Juvenile literature. 2. Survival after airplane accidents,
shipwrecks, etc. — Juvenile literature. I. Title. II. Series.
G525.O84 2009
613.6'9 — dc22
                                                2008034519

Summary: Describes tips for surviving being lost at sea.

Editorial Credits
Angie Kaelberer, editor; Veronica Bianchini, designer; Wanda Winch,
    photo researcher; Sarah L. Schuette, photo stylist; Marcy Morin, photo
    shoot scheduler

Photo Credits
Capstone Press/Karon Dubke, 11
Corbis/Royalty-Free, 9
Getty Images Inc./Frederick M. Brown, 7; Hulton Archive/General Photographic Agency, 20;
    Photographer's Choice/Eddie Soloway, 6
Minden Pictures/Hedgehog House/Colin Monteath, front cover
Rod Whigham, 19, 21, 23, 27
Shutterstock/Dennis Sabo, 25 (bottom); Jose Alberto Tejo, 14; Leo, 28; NatUlrich, 10;
    Sergey Popov V, 25 (top); toshimself, back cover, 4–5
U.S. Coast Guard Photo/CWO Jim Robertson, 29; Robin Ressler, PA2, 12–13

1 2 3 4 5 6 14 13 12 11 10 09

Table of Contents

Chapter 1

Water Everywhere

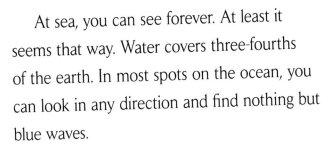

At sea, you can see forever. At least it seems that way. Water covers three-fourths of the earth. In most spots on the ocean, you can look in any direction and find nothing but blue waves.

If the day is sunny and you're traveling on a cozy boat, this is a pleasant picture. But not every day at sea is calm. Blue skies turn stormy. Wind whips water into dangerous waves. Even the largest ship can be swallowed by towering **hurricane** waves.

Other things can go wrong too. Enormous rogue waves
can roar out of nowhere and flood a ship. Captains sometimes
make mistakes. They could crash into other boats or scrape
an iceberg. Boats and ships can break down, leaving the
passengers stranded in the middle of the ocean.

If you're in any of these situations, you'll still probably
see nothing but water. But you'll be wishing for land! In
the meantime, you'll have to do what it takes to survive at sea.

DEBBIE KILEY: FIVE DAYS AT SEA

In 1982, Debbie Kiley was sailing in the Atlantic Ocean on a yacht with four other people. A hurricane sunk their yacht, leaving the five in an inflatable boat. The air was a chilly 40 degrees Fahrenheit (4 degrees Celsius). Debbie and her crewmates fought off hypothermia by huddling together and covering themselves with seaweed. They also warmed up in the ocean water, which was 76 degrees Fahrenheit (24 degrees Celsius). But they couldn't do that for long, because sharks often circled below their boat.

After three days, two of Kiley's friends gave into temptation and drank ocean water. They became too dehydrated to think clearly. Both jumped overboard and were killed by sharks.

On the fourth day, a third crewmate died from injuries. That left Kiley and Brad Cavanagh as the only survivors. They were rescued the next day by a Russian ship.

hypothermia – a medical condition that occurs when body temperature falls several degrees below normal

dehydration – a medical condition caused by a lack of water

A SALTY PROBLEM

The sea is an especially dangerous and frustrating place to be stranded. When you're stuck on an island or in a forest, you can search for water and food. You can build a shelter and make a fire to keep warm.

In the middle of the ocean, you can't do those things. Not easily, at least. It's possible to find food, if you can figure out a way to catch fish or birds. At the same time, you'll need to be careful of other sea creatures, especially sharks. You'll also have to deal with the weather. You'll need to protect yourself from the blistering sun and the brisk wind. If the water or air is cold, you'll have to try to prevent hypothermia.

The trickiest part of being stranded at sea is the water itself. Even though you're surrounded by water, you can't drink any of it. Ocean water is filled with salt. Drinking saltwater is extremely dangerous. If you drink a cup of ocean water, your body uses two cups of fluid to flush out the salt, which will dehydrate you. Dehydration keeps your brain from working correctly. And you'll need to be completely alert to survive until you're rescued.

There are ways to survive in the middle of the ocean, though. Read on to find out how.

MAKE A SURVIVAL KIT

Every boat should have life jackets, emergency flares, and fire extinguishers on board. It's also a good idea to bring your own survival kit. Here are some items to include:

- blankets
- bottled water
- canned or dried food
- can opener
- first-aid kit
- fishing line and hooks
- flashlight
- fresh batteries

- Global Positioning System (GPS)
- lip balm
- rope
- sealable plastic bags
- sextant
- sharp knife or scissors

- solar still or desalination kit
- sunscreen
- tarp
- two-way radio
- wet suit
- wool hat

Chapter 2

Stay Warm, Stay Dry, Survive!

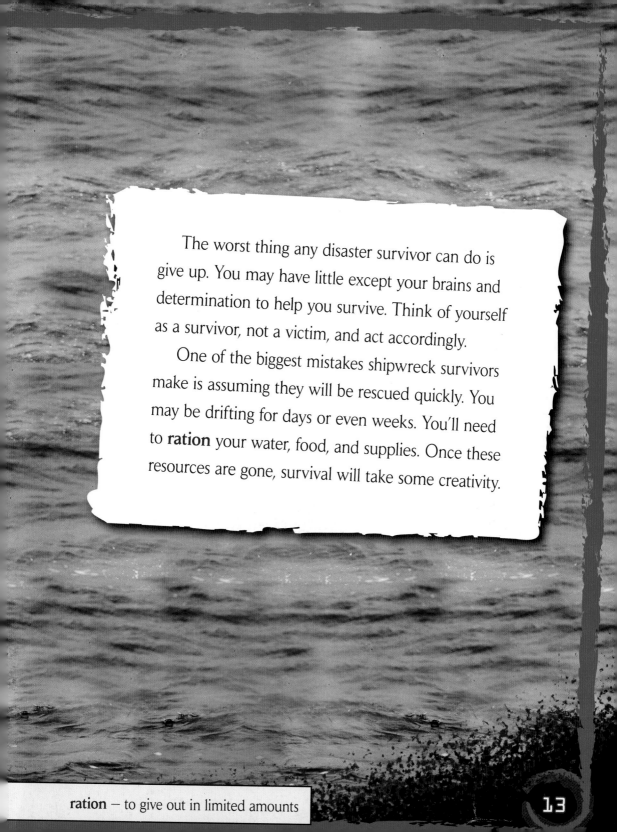

The worst thing any disaster survivor can do is give up. You may have little except your brains and determination to help you survive. Think of yourself as a survivor, not a victim, and act accordingly.

One of the biggest mistakes shipwreck survivors make is assuming they will be rescued quickly. You may be drifting for days or even weeks. You'll need to **ration** your water, food, and supplies. Once these resources are gone, survival will take some creativity.

How to

PREPARE FOR DISASTER

The moment you step on a watercraft, scope it out. Where are the lifeboats and life jackets? What materials are packed into the survival kits? Is bottled water easily available? If the boat starts to sink, what will you do?

Think about those things ahead of time. Practice what you would do if the boat sinks. If disaster strikes, you won't have a lot of time to think.

What if

YOUR SHIP SINKS?

In a sinking situation, you'll need to decide quickly whether to stay on the ship or escape in a lifeboat. It may seem obvious to jump into the lifeboat, but that's not always the best decision. Not every ship sinks completely. If yours is damaged but not sunk, you may be better off staying on it. Rescuers may have an easier time spotting you on the wreckage of the ship. Generally, you should choose to leave the ship when the water on the boat reaches your waist.

If you need to escape in a lifeboat, the situation will be stressful. Be sure to put on a life jacket and bring your drinking water. You can even throw plastic jugs of water overboard. They'll float, and you can pick them up later.

TIP: If the sinking ship's fuel spills into the water, get far away. Sparks from the ship could cause the water to catch fire.

GET WATER

Eventually, any fresh water you manage to take with you will run out. But getting a drink when you're surrounded by saltwater isn't impossible. If your lifeboat or survival kit has a desalination kit or a solar still, you're in luck. A desalination device pumps ocean water through a filter that removes the salt. The result is fresh water that you can safely drink.

You can make a solar still from a waterproof container, a cup, and a piece of clear plastic or glass. Place a cup of saltwater inside the container and cover the container with the clear plastic or glass. Place a rock on top of the lid to keep it from blowing off. In the sun, the fresh water slowly **evaporates**, leaving the salt behind. The drinkable water **condenses** on the plastic covering and runs down the inside of the container.

Without this equipment, your best chance of getting fresh water is rain. Use containers or a tarp to collect rainwater.

evaporate — to change a liquid into a gas
condense — to change a gas into a liquid

TIP: If you don't have drinkable water, don't eat. It will only make you thirstier. If you do have water, eat sweet foods, rather than salty ones.

How to

CATCH FOOD

Meat from fish and turtles is generally safe to eat. Stay away from colorful fish, though. Some of them are poisonous. In shallower waters, you might find lobsters, crab, and crayfish.

If you have fishing line and hooks, you're in luck. If not, think about things you can use to make a hook. Pieces of metal can be bent into a hook shape. Even a dangling earring could work.

For bait, you can use small bits of food. Be careful not to use too much. You may be better off saving that food for yourself. If you have a net or bucket, lower it into the water to catch tiny fish for bait. No net? Cut a wide slit in a plastic water jug.

If your boat floats long enough, algae and seaweed will grow on the underside. Fish will come up to the boat to feed on the plants. Use your net or even your hands to catch the fish. If you have a knife, attach it to a stick or pole. Use this weapon to spear fish.

Birds are another good source of food. If you have a net, try using it to catch birds that fly near your boat. You can use small pieces of food or small fish to attract them.

You probably won't be able to cook your food on a lifeboat. Eating raw meat usually isn't a good idea. It can contain bacteria that cooking would kill. But in a survival situation, sometimes you have to go for the gross.

TIP: A fish's fillet is found between the head and gills. With crabs, lobsters, and turtles, you'll need to crack through the shell to get to the edible part.

TRAGEDY OF THE *TITANIC*

When *Titanic* left Europe in April 1912, people called the ship unsinkable. But on its first voyage, the ship scraped against an iceberg. Within hours, it sank to the bottom of the Atlantic Ocean.

Titanic is often remembered for the more than 1,500 people who died on April 15, 1912. But another 705 people survived, and there probably could have been more.

Titanic's 20 lifeboats had a total of 1,178 seats, only enough for half the people on the ship. Officers lowered the first lifeboats before the seats were filled, partly because many people refused to leave the ship.

When the ship filled with water, it split into two pieces. Many passengers were thrown overboard. Most of the people in the water died quickly of hypothermia. Lifeboats rowed away from the wreckage, so they wouldn't be sucked down with the sinking ship. Only one lifeboat went back to search for survivors. Very few were found.

People in the lifeboats huddled together to stay warm. Two hours after the sinking, the ship *Carpathia* arrived to rescue the survivors.

Titanic survivors huddled in a lifeboat.

RELIEVE YOURSELF

Lifeboats don't have toilets. You'll have to figure out the safest way to do your business.

If you jump into the water to relieve yourself, you run the risk of attracting sharks. These predators are drawn to the odor of human waste. If you relieve yourself inside the boat, you may catch diseases from the germs.

The best option is to use a container or plastic bag while on the boat. Then rinse it out in the water. The second-best option is to relieve yourself over the side of the boat. Attach a rope to the inside of the boat, and hold onto it while you lean over the side.

PREVENT HYPOTHERMIA

Staying warm at sea isn't just a matter of comfort. It can mean the difference between life and death. If your body temperature drops below 95 degrees Fahrenheit (35 degrees Celsius), you can develop hypothermia.

The first step to avoiding hypothermia is getting out of the water. The only exception is if the water is warmer than the air. This is often true in the **Gulf Stream**. If you have to stay in the water, stay still. Staying still will lessen the amount of body heat you'll lose. It also makes you less likely to attract sharks.

Whether you're in the water or on a boat, you lose a large amount of heat through the head. Wearing a wool cap will help. You also lose heat through your neck, arms, and groin. Cover those areas with blankets, clothing, or seaweed.

If you're alone, pull your knees tightly to your chest to keep warm. If you are with others, huddle together to share body heat.

Gulf Stream — a warm current in the Atlantic Ocean

TIP: In water that is 50 degrees Fahrenheit (10 degrees Celsius), you will show signs of hypothermia after an hour. But in a wet suit, you can make it 10 hours before hypothermia kicks in.

How to

BEAT THE WEATHER

A lifeboat provides little or no protection from the weather. Sun and wind burn your skin and increase dehydration. Cold, pounding rain can cause hypothermia.

Take a look at the tools you have available and be creative. Does the lifeboat have a tarp covering? Use that to protect yourself from sun and rain. Do you have extra clothing? Drape it over your head and face to protect them from sunburn. If you catch a bird for food, you can rub the fat on your skin. It sounds gross, but the slimy fat is a good sunscreen.

THEY STING AND BITE!

People often worry about shark attacks in ocean waters. But other sea creatures are dangerous too.

Both jellyfish and barracuda will attack people who get in their way. Some types of jellyfish are harmless. Others have deadlier venom than poisonous snakes do.

Barracuda can be 6 feet (1.8 meters) long. They can weigh 100 pounds (45 kilograms). They use their razorlike teeth to catch and kill prey.

The best way to avoid these critters is to stay out of the water. When you have to be in the water, watch for them. Most jellyfish are rubbery, see-through blobs. Barracuda are tougher to spot because they move fast. If you do see a barracuda, face it and move toward it. It will probably swim away.

Jellyfish

If you are bitten or stung, treat the wound quickly. Wash a barracuda bite and bandage it. Apply pressure to the bite to stop the bleeding. If a jellyfish stings you, rinse the wound with saltwater. Then wash the area with vinegar, if you have it. Vinegar helps keep the venom from spreading through your body. Finally, use a cloth to remove any tentacles stuck to your skin.

Barracuda

How to

AVOID SHARKS

Sharks usually attack people by mistake. Most shark attacks involve only one bite. But that bite can be deadly.

Remember the things that attract sharks. They can smell blood from long distances. Sharks also can see shiny jewelry and brightly colored swimsuits. Even the contrast between light and dark tan lines may get a shark's attention. If you have to go in the water, take off any jewelry and wear dark clothes.

Sharks are more likely to attack an individual person than a group of people swimming together. You're also more likely to be attacked if you're floating on the surface. To a shark, you'll look like food.

Remaining in your lifeboat is a good idea, but it doesn't completely protect you from a shark. Shark skin is razor-sharp. If it scrapes an inflatable boat, it can cause leaks. You can decrease the chances of a shark visit by not throwing food scraps overboard.

If you do find yourself face to face with a shark, hit it in the eyes or the gills. A shark is most sensitive in these areas. If you can't reach those, then aim for the nose. But don't stick around for a 12-round boxing match! Get away as quickly as you can.

TIP: When trying to escape a shark, swim away as smoothly as possible. Moving and splashing will only attract the shark's attention.

What if

YOU SEE A PLANE OR SHIP

If you're lost at sea, one of the most exciting things is the sight of a ship or an airplane. One of the deepest disappointments is the sight of it passing you by.

To people aboard a plane or ship, your tiny lifeboat may be barely noticeable. You need signals that will grab their attention. Flares that shoot fire and smoke into the sky work very well. A flashlight shining into the night sky may do the trick too. During the day, you can use shiny objects like watches, jewelry, mirrors, or aluminum to reflect sunlight and create a glare.

If you have a radio, use it to alert the airplane or ship. You'll probably have to try several frequencies to find the right channel. If you do get in touch, indicate you need help by using the word "Mayday."

Flare gun and flares

SURVIVING AT SEA

Ever since the first explorers traveled by water, people have been stuck at sea. Many have died. But others have survived by being disciplined and making smart choices. They used their supplies carefully. They creatively found ways to get food and drinkable water.

People who survive the sea are a little lucky. But living long enough to be rescued doesn't just take luck. It takes the courage to face a horrible situation and make the decision to survive.

Glossary

barracuda (ba-ruh-KOO-duh) — a fish with a long, narrow body and many sharp teeth

condense (kuhn-DENS) — to change from gas to liquid; water vapor condenses into liquid water.

dehydration (dee-hy-DRAY-shuhn) — a life-threatening medical condition caused by a lack of water

desalination (dee-sah-luh-NAY-shuhn) — the process of removing the salt from ocean water

evaporate (i-VA-puh-rayt) — to change from a liquid into a gas

Gulf Stream (GUHLF STREEM) — a warm current flowing in the Atlantic Ocean from the Gulf of Mexico up the eastern U.S. coast

hurricane (HUR-uh-kane) — a very large storm with high winds and rain; hurricanes form over warm ocean water.

hypothermia (hye-puh-THUR-mee-uh) — a life-threatening medical condition resulting from a drop in body temperature

ration (RASH-uhn) — to give out in limited amounts

rogue wave (ROHG WAYV) — a giant, unexpected wave that can be as tall as 100 feet (30 meters)

tentacle (TEN-tuh-kuhl) — a thin, flexible arm on some animals

yacht (YAHT) — a large boat used for sailing or racing

Read More

Lewis, Simon. *Survival at Sea.* Difficult and Dangerous. Mankato, Minn.: Black Rabbit Books, 2009.

O'Shei, Tim. *Shipwreck!: Debbie Kiley's Story of Survival.* True Tales of Survival. Mankato, Minn.: Capstone Press, 2008.

Porterfield, Jason. *Shipwreck: True Stories of Survival.* Survivor Stories. New York: Rosen, 2006.

Woods, Michael, and Mary B. Woods. *Disasters at Sea.* Disasters Up Close. Minneapolis: Lerner, 2008.

Internet Sites

FactHound offers a safe, fun way to find educator-approved Internet sites related to this book.

Here's what you do:

1. Visit *www.facthound.com*
2. Choose your grade level.
3. Begin your search.

This book's ID number is 9781429622806.

FactHound will fetch the best sites for you!

Index